KITSUNE

JAPAN'S SHAPESHIFTING TRICKSTERS

by Elizabeth Andrews

abdobooks.com

Published by Pop!, a division of ABDO, PO Box 398166, Minneapolis, Minnesota 55439. Copyright © 2023 by Abdo Consulting Group, Inc. International copyrights reserved in all countries. No part of this book may be reproduced in any form without written permission from the publisher. DiscoverRoo™ is a trademark and logo of Pop!.

Printed in the United States of America, North Mankato, Minnesota.

052022
092022

THIS BOOK CONTAINS RECYCLED MATERIALS

Cover Photo: Shutterstock Images

Interior Photos: Shutterstock Images, Brooklyn Museum, Bequest of Grace M. Pugh, 1985

Editor: Bridget O'Brien
Series Designer: Laura Graphenteen

Library of Congress Control Number: 2021951847

Publisher's Cataloging-in-Publication Data

Names: Andrews, Elizabeth, author.

Title: Kitsune: Japan's shapeshifting tricksters / by Elizabeth Andrews

Other title: Japan's shapeshifting tricksters

Description: Minneapolis, Minnesota : Pop, 2023 | Series: Creatures of legend | Includes online resources and index

Identifiers: ISBN 9781098242343 (lib. bdg.) | ISBN 9781098243043 (ebook)

Subjects: LCSH: Tricksters--Asia, Central--Juvenile literature. | Monsters--Juvenile literature. | Animals-- Folklore--Juvenile literature. | Fabled creatures-- Juvenile literature.

Classification: DDC 001.944--dc23

WELCOME TO DiscoverRoo!

Pop open this book and you'll find QR codes loaded with information, so you can learn even more!

Scan this code* and others like it while you read, or visit the website below to make this book pop!

popbooksonline.com/kitsune

*Scanning QR codes requires a web-enabled smart device with a QR code reader app and a camera.

TABLE OF CONTENTS

CHAPTER 1

BEWARE THE WEARY TRAVELER

An old man walks down a dark and rainy road in Japan. He is hunched over and looks worse for wear. A younger, healthy man stops to check on him. The old man has been traveling for a long time. He

Kitsune usually target people who are alone.

is tired and cold. He hasn't had a warm

meal in days. The younger man wants

to help.

So, the young man invites the old
man to his home. He makes him tea and
gives him dry clothes and warm food. The
young man lets his guest spend the night.

Tea in Japan is served in cups without handles.

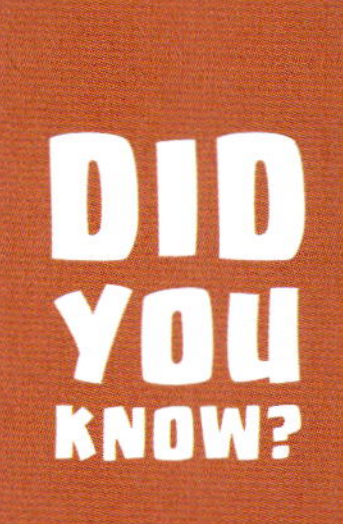

When morning comes, the young man wakes to a terrible scene. All his possessions are gone and so is the old man. When he places his hand to his head in surprise, he feels bare skin. His hair had been shaved! The young man knows exactly what has happened. He's fallen for a kitsune's tricks.

CLEVER AS A FOX

Japanese people used to live alongside wildlife. The country was **rural**, and most people were farmers. Foxes were a common animal to see. They caused trouble for the people of Japan by eating the small animals that farmers kept. Foxes hunt in the simplest way. A bunch of well-fed chickens rounded up in a pen

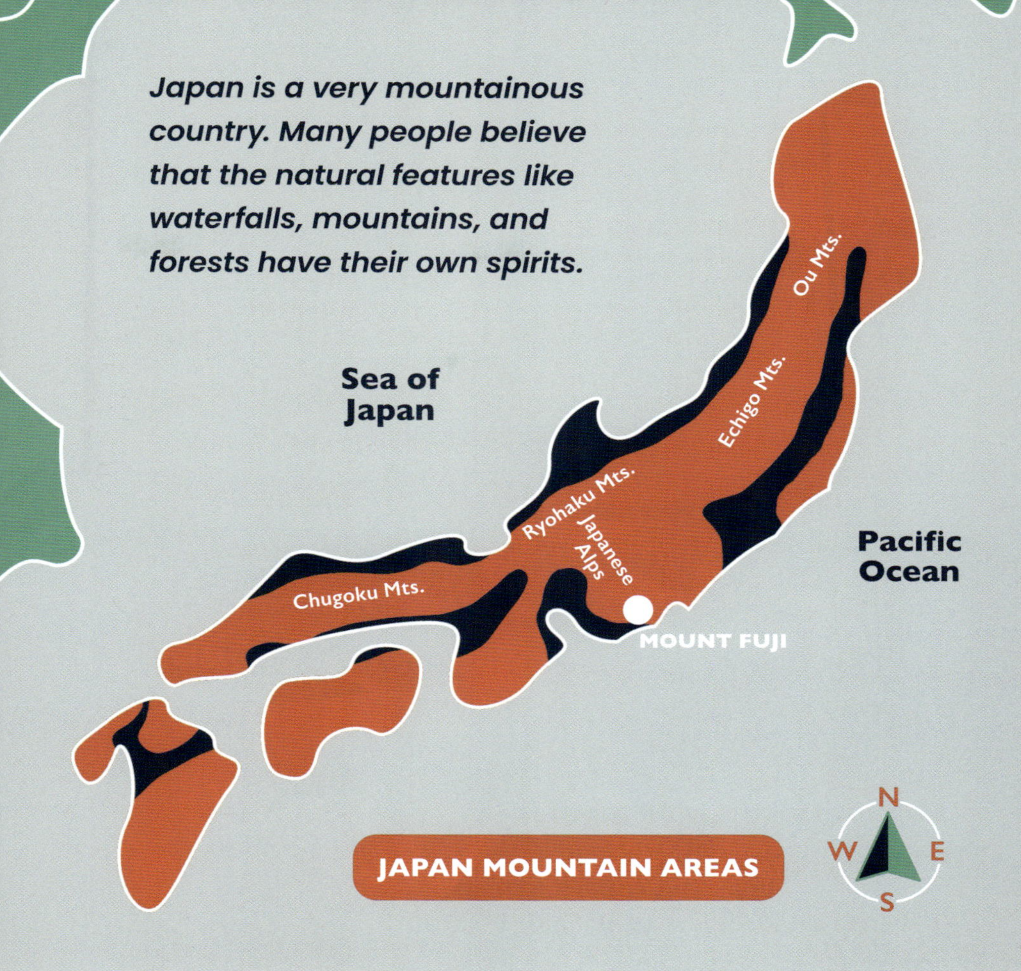

would be an easy meal for the fox. This kind of behavior inspired the stories of naughty kitsune.

Seeing a white kitsune is a sign that good things will happen.

Kitsune are very smart foxes that have **supernatural** abilities. There are many kinds of kitsune. Some are divine helpers. Others are mischievous troublemakers. This legendary creature earned many of its traits from the fox.

KITSUNE WEDDINGS

In Japan, there is a legend about kitsune weddings. It began as an explanation for sun showers and ghost lights. Ghost lights are sometimes called will-o'-the-wisps. People believe that when they witness the lights and sun showers, there is a kitsune wedding happening nearby. It means good luck. The legend has inspired festivals in Japan.

The **deity** Inari is the protector of foxes. Inari's appearance differs from story to story. Sometimes Inari is a bearded man riding a white fox. Other times, Inari is a beautiful woman carrying rice. Inari is also the god of **prosperity**, rice, and tea. Rice was the most important food in Japan, so people took worship of Inari very seriously.

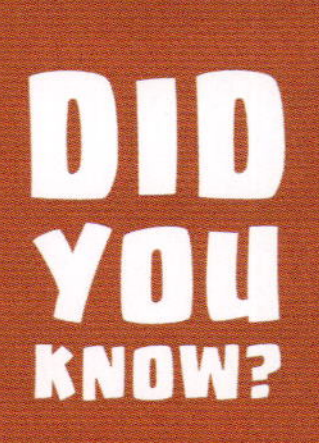

Shrines of Inari are decorated with kitsune statues. The statues often have red scarves to help protect against evil.

More than one third of
the shrines in Japan
are dedicated to Inari.

It was believed that kitsune were the messengers for this deity. They could travel between the human and the spirit worlds. Kitsune stood guard at **portals** that lead to and from the spirit world. A fox's burrow was thought to be a portal.

While foxes caused trouble and chaos from time to time, people treated them with respect. Every fox was assumed

Foxes make many different sounds. Some sound like laughter and screaming.

to be a servant of Inari. This meant they could be extremely powerful. The power they had could be used to either harm or help any human they encountered.

CHAPTER 3

SKILLS OF THE KITSUNE

Kitsune can live for a very long time.

Some live to be 1,000 years old. Every 100 years, a kitsune grows a new tail. The more tails a kitsune has, the more powerful it is. The most tails a kitsune can have is nine. Each time it grows a new tail, it gains more knowledge, like languages, and magical abilities.

A nine-tailed kitsune can see and hear everything happening in the world. It is the most powerful form of the creature.

Kitsune are shape shifters. They get better at it as they age. A kitsune with just one tail might not be able to change more than its coat color. Eventually a kitsune will be able to transform into a human. It can use this ability for good or for bad.

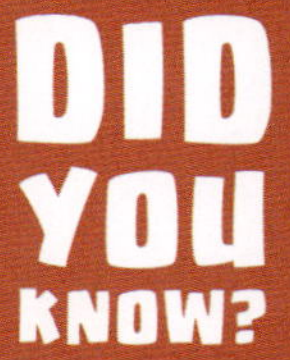

The only way to kill a kitsune is to cut off all its tails.

The best time to catch sight of
a fox is dawn or dusk.

Kitsune often take the shape of
women. They can make
powerful men fall in
love with them in
this shape.

Troublesome kitsune use their shape shifting ability to benefit themselves. Like in the story from chapter one, they can change into humans in need to get invited into people's homes. Kitsune in human form may also lead travelers astray. Their reasoning for playing these tricks could be for something as simple as being woken up from a nap.

Another skill a kitsune gains with age

is the power of **illusion**. A kitsune can

make a person believe they are seeing

entire cities. A human under the control

of a kitsune's illusion might walk for miles

thinking they are on a beautiful, wooded

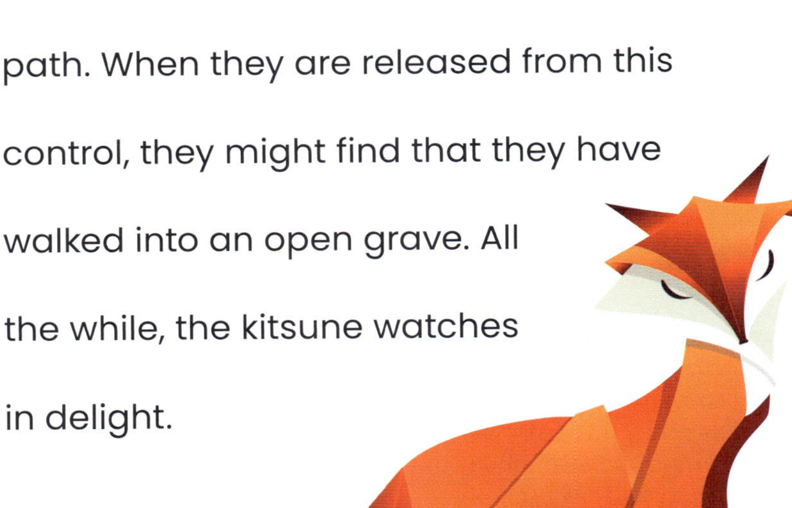

path. When they are released from this

control, they might find that they have

walked into an open grave. All

the while, the kitsune watches

in delight.

CHAPTER 4

PROTECTING AGAINST KITSUNE

Humans must stay aware to protect themselves against kitsune. Kitsune can **possess** humans once they reach a certain level of power. A kitsune usually chooses to possess a person if they wronged the kitsune in some way. This

It is safest to assume that every fox is a kitsune.

could have happened because a human

accidentally killed a kitsune's baby or

disturbed a den.

There are many stories of kitsune possessing pretty young women.

The kitsune usually works its spirit into the body of the human through the fingernails. The human knows it is possessed because it can hear the kitsune's thoughts. But the kitsune has full control of the human's body. It will speak for them. A kitsune loves to cause chaos when it's possessing a body. It will force the person to appear mad by running through the streets barking at people and starting fights.

DID YOU KNOW?

When a person is possessed by a kitsune, their face may change to look a bit fox-like.

Kitsune are very protective of their tails.

There are ways to know if a person

is possessed by a kitsune or if a kitsune

is disguised as a human. The person will

glow. If it's dark out, the person will still

appear clearly. A kitsune who has shape

shifted may have a reflection that shows

a tail or ears. This isn't true for all kitsune in disguise, but younger ones may not be powerful enough to keep themselves hidden. Their shadows will always be that of a fox as well.

The people of Japan take steps to always protect themselves from kitsune. Since all kitsune are afraid of dogs, many people keep a dog as a pet. A kitsune in disguise won't enter a home if there is a dog there. Some people may also keep a dog tooth in their pockets. This protects them against any possible possession.

TEXT-TO-SELF

Do you think you would fall for a kitsune's illusion? Why or why not?

TEXT-TO-TEXT

Have you read any other books about a legendary creature? How were the creatures in those books similar to and different from the kitsune?

TEXT-TO-WORLD

The Japanese are very hospitable people. Do you know of any other cultures that take pride in their hospitality?

GLOSSARY

deity — a god or goddess.

hospitable — friendly, giving, and warm to guests.

illusion — something that is not real but that seems to be true or real.

portal — an entrance to a place.

possess — to enter into and control someone.

prosperity — the condition of being successful or thriving.

rural — having to do with country life.

supernatural — something that exists beyond what is observable.

INDEX

ONLINE RESOURCES
popbooksonline.com

Scan this code* and others like it while you read, or visit the website below to make this book pop!

popbooksonline.com/kitsune

*Scanning QR codes requires a web-enabled smart device with a QR code reader app and a camera.